Preparing the HEART for Ministry

"Vessel Preparation"

By Evangelist/CoPastor Cynthia L. Butler

Xulon PRESS

Preparing the HEART for Ministry Vessel Preparation
by Evangelist/CoPastor Cynthia L. Butler

Printed in the United States of America

ISBN 9781609570835

Unless otherwise indicated, Bible quotations are taken from The King James Version of the Bible.

www.xulonpress.com

Table of Contents

-realize that blame is a coward's way of dealing
  with the past

-taking responsibility for our part of our history

-no longer being ruled by people and incidents
  of the past

-releasing from the bondage of unforgiveness

-seeking the Lord for our area of ministry

-total surrender to God's instructions and directions

-taking the limits off what we will/can do for God

-giving God the issues of submission

Introduction

Where ever men and women are found seeking to please the Lord there you'll find a need for basic spiritual growth principles. As a ministry workshop for women was developing in our church, there was a need for curriculum that would become a foundation for souls seeking to move into their calling and/or area of ministry.

This book was originally designed for that particular women's ministry workshop curriculum. As the writing and research progressed the word "women" was removed because of a realization that all vessels seeking to please God really needed these types of principles. Every soul that lives for God must connect to the "study to show thyself approved" instruction in 2 Timothy.

2 Tim 2:14-15 Of these things put them in remembrance, charging them before the Lord that they strive not about words to no profit, but to the subverting of the hearers.

15 Study to shew thyself approved unto God, a workman that needeth not to be ashamed, rightly dividing the word of truth. KJV

The note of this scripture in verse fifteen particularly is that we be reminded that this is a "charge," a command and direct instruction from Christ, that we learn, rehearse and practice the instructions and directives of the word of God. God knows that we need to have a lifelong commitment to lifelong learning of Him! No casual or part time student of the word of God will be able to stand before God and be approved in the presence of his perfection. It also stands as a reminder that there is no vanity in the word of God. Those who choose confusing jargon, extensive vocabularies, and unknown or mysterious revelations will be no more approved before the "all knowing" God than a stranger to the word and ways of God would be. God wants us to remember how enormously intelligent he is.

The more experiences in ministry I have the more I have found that many souls are lacking foundational truths in their spirits and hearts. It was as if many people skipped the basic training of the gospels; grades one through three in education. Those academic developmental years provide foundation for all future learning experiences and lessons. This is relayed in many formats but one that I recall the most is a book that came out years ago that proved that kindergarten learning was the foundation to all basics for life. Some sincere believers may have skipped the basics of salvation and sanctification, skipping a couple of spiritual growth years. Although some may have giftedness that opens doors from the spiritual crib to powerful ministry, those formative years also provide social and emotional development lessons that often glue our spiritual gifts to godly standards that help us survive ministry level storms. When people skip the basics, grades one through three, and leap into upper grades without the basic knowledge they need to continually progress and grow in God, it is a formula for failure.

I have had very smart students who were academically above grade level, but under-developed social behaviors and emotional immaturity wreaked havoc on them. They struggled to "fit in", make friends, or just to play like other children their age. The lessons of sharing and play from preschool to kindergarten, the lessons of grouping and categorizing from kindergarten to first grade, and the first grade instructions in reading, comprehension and computations are interwoven in lessons in all areas and levels thereafter. It would then be important to deduct that those missing lessons may need to be inserted and learned somewhere else along the way. There are many principles social, emotional and academic in our spiritual growth that may need to be inserted to balance and secure us in our purpose and ministry assignments current and prophetic.

This book is not to answer all the questions or insert all the lessons missed or missing. It is just a reference to the basics that every believer should review and investigate as we grow in the grace and knowledge of our Lord Jesus Christ. In truth only the Word of God is the complete book of answers. This book is simply another tool usable to those doing spiritual maintenance; checking to see that God is pleased with the presentation of their lives before him.

When I needed these principles I had to piece them together from messages from other presenters, bible study, Sunday school lessons and asking many questions to those I felt were able to mentor and counsel me. Unfortunately, most of what I have learned was through trial and error… many trials and many errors. My prayer is that I can help someone avoid as many errors as I have made through these lessons and revelations of basic salvation and sanctification.

I prayerfully submit this work of my hands and heart before God, that God will approve and believers will be blessed with the basic knowledge needed for progressive and impacting spiritual growth. I pray that you read and grow thereby, IN JESUS' NAME. AMEN!

Submitted in Love by your sister in Christ and fellow seeker, Sister Cynthia.

Part 1

A.

The Heart that faces truth about the past.

-realize that blame is a coward's way of dealing with the
 past
-taking responsibility for our part of our history

"The Blame Game"

To blame is to account cause to a bad/negative situation. The first example that comes to mind is that of Adam and Eve. When God addressed their sinful act of disobedience in the garden Adam blamed Eve and Eve blamed the serpent. The environment of blame only caused the sin to be magnified. (See Genesis 3:11-13).

"I wonder if the curse in Genesis 3:14-24 would have been any different had blame been replaced with open acknowledgment and humble repentance."

How many times does a parent tell his/her little child to just tell the truth and the consequences would not be more lenient? How often have you wished that someone would have just said he/she was sorry instead of making excuses or blaming something or someone for what happened? Blame moves negative situations in directions opposite of healing and resolution.

Blame – to say that someone is/or the cause of something bad. (Webster's dictionary)

The truth of the Adam and Eve situation is that God knew what happened, he must have desired more than blame as a response. He asked who told them that they were naked. It seemed to be more of a rhetorical question; asking just to make them aware of who just deceived them. Perhaps he desired a confession of sin and repentance of the failure. If we are to be freed from the bondage of our sins, mistakes and failures we must be willing to just face the fact that it happened, repent of it and turn from our wicked ways and not do it again. Godly sorrow worketh repentance.

"We can't be godly sorry if we are only sorry that we got caught."

We need to realize that each of our sins and failures hurts God's heart.

2 Corinthians 7:9-10 Now I rejoice, not that ye were made sorry, but that ye sorrowed to repentance: for ye were made sorry after a godly manner, that ye might receive damage by us in nothing. 10 For godly sorrow worketh repentance to salvation not to be repented of: but the sorrow of the world worketh death. KJV

Paul was speaking to the church at Corinth about the power of repentance. He was happy that his letter to them was all they needed to be sorry and repent to God.

"Salvation came to the people who received the revelation of their sin and responded with a HEART of repentance."

He most visibly wanted to demonstrate that repentance is provoked by godly sorrow. David spoke often in the book of Psalms to the Lord saying… "I have sinned against thee and thee only."

Psalms 41:4 I said, LORD, be merciful unto me: heal my soul; for I have sinned against thee. KJV

No blame is necessary for hearts whose desire is to live pleasing to the Father.

"When God's displeasure is revealed, the appropriate response is "Father, I have sinned against thee and thee only."

I was in the wrong place, doing the wrong thing, in the midst of the wrong people. I let the enemy deceive me and use me, Lord I just wouldn't let it go and I am sorry." This is a true confession and it blames no one but self and flesh. The key to true repentance is that no matter what the cause or blame, let it go and take responsibility for your failure before God and let God forgive, heal and deliver your HEART.

THE HEART OF MINISTRY = YOUR WILL!

There is something powerful about the HEART. It is more than the muscle that pumps blood throughout your body. It is more than your emotions. It's more than your desires. The HEART is your intentions and the areas and subjects where you are willing to submit and humble yourself before God. The HEART here speaks of your "Will" which is a composite of the principles that you center and initiate your actions from.

Ps 139:23-24 Search me, O God, and know my heart: try me, and know my thoughts: 24 And see if there be any wicked way in me, and lead me in the way everlasting. KJV

We cannot trust ourselves with a self-evaluation of our HEARTS.

"God is the pure examiner of things that are true and pertinent to our current conditions."

He has no underlying agenda or need to condemn us to make himself look better. His every action and intention is that we be saved and righteous as he is righteous.

When we look at our own heart, or have others evaluate our hearts, we may encounter partiality and bias just by our nature. God will be a timely and thorough analyst of the affairs of the heart. Out part is to "will" it; giving God permission, through obedience and submission, to deal with our hearts.

"Surrendering our will to God ultimately means that we will not resist or rebel against what God reveals and require of us."

Rather, we will open ourselves to the deliverance that the revelation/truth is designed to perform in us. When we submit to the power of the truth of God we open our lives to God. His loving healing and altering deliverance will begin to move throughout our hearts and transform us into the "good" that God has for us to experience and possess.

Rom 7:18 For I know that in me (that is, in my flesh,) dwelleth no good thing: for to will is present with me; but how to perform that which is good I find not. KJV

We are not set free just by knowledge or knowing about sin because our minds cannot free us. It takes the power of God to set us free. Our intellect is a tool to awaken us to the need for deliverance. But intelligence alone cannot deliver us. We have no spiritual basis to perform the good (the deliverance) needed in ourselves. We must therefore have our "will" or willingness surrendered to allow God's intervention to set us free and work in us.

"His power alone can break chains that have clinched our wrists like handcuffs from our child-hood even until now."

God requires our will to be free, but then he will move in great power and make things happen on our behalf. (See Philippians 2:13)

Phil 2:12-13 Wherefore, my beloved, as ye have always obeyed, not as in my presence only, but now much more in my absence, work out your own salvation with fear and trembling. 13 For it is God which worketh in you both to will and to do of his good pleasure. KJV

There may be things that God will not choose to reveal to us, but by yielding our will to him it will allow him to cleanse and heal us from all that causes us not to be approved of him. His great wisdom may dictate a need for us to just trust Him to know what is best for us. This may mean that some things we may never know or understand why or what. We may be like the blind man who testified in the temple who in essence said, "I don't know what happened.

"All I know is that I once was blind, but now I see."

I don't know that God promises us to explain things, but he did promise to work all things together for our good. We have to trust God. Trust that he knows what is best for us. No matter how horrific or tragic our past, God can and will fix it so it helps us be what he wants us to be in the end. Many pains and problems of my past have become my greatest areas of ministry. God turned it around. Failures once predicted my future but God took them and taught me about them; how they came about. He often teaches me why I was opened to those failures, what spirit or tool of the enemy was used against me.

"Best of all he gives me a word and promise to place in my HEART so that I never will be slave to those failures again."

THE HEART OF MINISTRY = THE CONDITION WHERE GOD CAUSES CHANGE SO WE CAN BE USED.

Ps 37:3-7 Trust in the LORD, and do good; so shalt thou dwell in the land, and verily thou shalt be fed. 4 Delight thyself also in the LORD; and he shall give thee the desires of thine heart. 5 Commit thy way unto the LORD; trust also in him; and he shall bring it to pass. 6 And he shall bring forth thy righteousness as the light, and thy judgment as the noonday. 7 Rest in the LORD, and wait patiently for him: fret not thyself because of him who prospereth in his way, because of the man who bringeth wicked devices to pass. KJV

This scripture reveals a stage of total trust in God and allowing him to do what is best for us. The "rest" in the Lord concept is just the position a trusting heart takes. It relaxes and has confidence that whatever the end of the matter, it will be good and in the purpose of God. This stage is where God will "lead me in the way everlasting." I pray that we all gain HEARTS that allow God to lead us into approval status on earth and eternal life.

THE HEART OF MINISTRY = THE PLACE OF TRUSTING GOD

B.

The Heart that forgives and is released from the past.

-is no longer being ruled by people and incidents of the past
-releasing from the bondage of unforgiveness and become free to be forgiven by the Father

Release from the offense and the offender

It's true.

"We can live no longer ruled by incidents and people of our past experiences."

We can possess forgiveness from the offense and the offender and be completely free.

2 Cor 2:5-11 But if any have caused grief, he hath not grieved me, but in part: that I may not overcharge you all. 6 Sufficient to such a man is this punishment, which was inflicted of many. 7 So that contrariwise ye ought rather to forgive him, and comfort him, lest perhaps such a one should be swallowed up with overmuch sorrow. 8 Wherefore I beseech you that ye would confirm your love toward him. 9 For to this end also did I write, that I might know the proof of you, whether ye be obedient in all things. 10 To whom ye forgive any thing, I forgive also: for if I forgave any thing, to whom I forgave it, for your sakes forgave I it in the person of Christ; 11 Lest Satan should get an advantage of us: for we are not ignorant of his devices. KJV

In this passage of scripture the offender had insulted the church specifically. The church members wanted Paul to punish the man for what he did. As the apostle, Paul let them know that he was offended but the greater offense was against the church. Therefore he instructed the local leaders of the church to handle the situation.

"He let them know that how they handled it will be an indicator of their level of obedience and spiritual growth."

He seemed to urge them to realize that the offense may become small in the light of the way they handle the situation. Verse six says that they might want to consider the grief of the offender from being brought before the church having the church have to deal with him. Paul said if I forgive him that would be good, but the offense was to the church and they need to forgive him, because they were offended. Paul said if I forgive him I would have to do it on your behalf and as a representative of Christ.

He made it clear that those who are offended must deal with the offense in total forgiveness. Likewise the offended soul needs to address the offender personally. Sometimes it is not possible or profitable to do that face to face. For instance it may be a whole group offense, like prejudice laws against a race or group of a certain economic status. It would be more profitable for individuals to forgive in their own heart rather than demand that every member of a large group come before them to be individually forgiven. It is also not possible when the offender is unreachable or no longer alive.

"Forgiveness is a process within our own heart."

Whether verbal confrontation is possible or not, true forgiveness happens in our hearts. If you were or are the one offended and hurt, face the offense in the name of Jesus and release the hurt, resentment and revenge against the offender and be free. Freedom comes through forgiving. Refuse to be ruled and manipulated by the ugly actions of an offender.

"The truth is that as long as we carry hurt, resentment, anger and unforgiveness towards the offender, that person or incident has power over us to continue to make us feel small and rejected."

Releasing forgiveness onto our offenders gives us back the power to live without guilt, hatred and condemnation. It also places that offender in God's court for justice as God sees fit. Free your HEART through forgiving.

"Forgive and release the power of God over your life to forgive you of your sins, mistakes and wrong intentions."

Face your offender with forgiveness. Then you no longer are responsible to punish or judge. The punishment judgment is then left in God's hands. You become free from the agony of offenses and the torment of injustice towards you. Satan no longer can use your unforgiveness as a device against your peace and right standing in Christ. Verse seven expresses it this way; "Lest Satan should get an advantage of us: for we are not ignorant of his devices." God frees us through forgiveness. On the contrary unforgiveness is a device of bondage that Satan often uses to keep us in anger, revenge and resentment.

"Unforgiveness is sin. God wants us to know that sin can come between you and God and severe your relationship ties".

Unforgiveness breaks up your relationship with God.

Isa 59:1-2 Behold, the LORD's hand is not shortened, that it cannot save; neither his ear heavy, that it cannot hear: 2 But your iniquities have separated between you and your God, and your sins have hid his face from you, that he will not hear. KJV

Then likewise, unforgiveness comes between you and God. So much that if you do not forgive, your father in heaven cannot forgive you. God has set a rule and guide to true forgiveness and freedom in him. Forgive!

Mark 11:25-26 And when ye stand praying, forgive, if ye have ought against any: that your Father also which is in heaven may forgive you your trespasses. 26 But if ye do not forgive, neither will your Father which is in heaven forgive your trespasses. KJV

Forgive and you are left free to live your life and move forward and that's what you really need to have instead of revenge.

"You need to get your life back."

Your HEART is the place of beginning new life after abuse, hurt and offense through forgiving.

THE HEART OF MINISTRY = THE POWER OF FREEDOM THROUGH FORGIVENESS

Even as God has forgiven you and provided forgiveness for you, release the offenses of your past, present, and future. Seek the Lord for a forgiving spirit, one that quickly forgives and holds no grudges. God has made provision through his word to give you a heart just like that. David demonstrated how to petition God for a forgiving heart.

Ps 51:10 Create in me a clean heart, O God; and renew a right spirit within me. KJV

Take a look at the lesson of forgiveness found in Matthew 18:21-35. In particular you'll find there the lord whose unforgiving spirit caused him to be delivered into the hand of the tormentors.

"He was not motivated by the forgiveness he received to become forgiving."

His unforgiveness brought him to a hopeless place in his life. He was condemned to prison until he could pay off the debt. It was a situation where this was a debt that required him to be rich or able to work off. The cycle of torment was unending not only by the fact that he needed to be free to be able to work to pay off the debt, but also because of the extreme torment forthcoming that was the reputation of the prison tormentors of the time.

Let your HEART be a place of divine advocacy through the power and spirit of forgiveness.

For further discussion see:
Matthew 6:14-15; Hebrews 10:26; Colossians 3:13; Proverbs 23:7

Notes:

C.

Pause for a study on "Forgiveness"

Forgiveness is a constant battle for those who choose to please God. Our daily activities place us in the path of unjust acts of men that often develop into areas of unforgiveness.

"In other words, people are always doing stuff to us that make us need to forgive them."

Forgiveness sometimes comes easy because we are sure that there was a mistake made or the act was unintended. Yet, even those unintentional acts may be challenging for many.

The greatest challenge of forgiveness is easily agreed to be those incidents that were intentional, done on purpose to hurt us or a blatant misuse of power over us. But it is a commandment from God that we forgive.

"Forgiveness may require brave and conscious efforts on our part, but in those efforts abides our access to forgiveness from God. "

Therefore we must forgive; for heaven's sake.

WHEN YOU HURT ~ FORGIVE!
WHEN YOU'RE MISTREATED~FORGIVE!
WHEN IT WASN'T YOUR FAULT~FORGIVE~
~FORGIVE!~~FORGIVE!~~FORGIVE!~~FORGIVE!~
~FORGIVE!~

Forgive – 1. To give up resentment against or the desire to punish; to stop being angry with; to pardon. 2. To give up all claim to punish or exact penalty for (an offense); to overlook
Forgive – to show forgiveness; to be inclined to forgive.
Forgiveness – Disposition to pardon; willingness to forgive (Webster)

Forgiving isn't just the great move of humility to overlook something; it is your inclination or your <u>will</u> to forgive.

"Once you choose to forgive the process is put into motion and the end is forgiveness."

"Lord I choose to forgive."

Mark 11:25-26 And when ye stand praying, forgive, if ye have ought against any: that your Father also which is in heaven may forgive you your trespasses. 26 But if ye do not forgive, neither will your Father which is in heaven forgive your trespasses. KJV

Mark helps us and motivates us to forgive by direct expression of the truth of God's rule on forgiveness as stated in verse twenty six. If we do not forgive, neither will God forgive us.

"It leaves us with no wiggle space, we must forgive."

Our willingness to forgive allows God to forgive us for our mistakes and failures. Thereby we should always keep our door for forgiveness from the Father wide opened. We ourselves must forgive unlimited and unconditionally.

THE HEART OF MINISTRY = EMPOWERED TO FORGIVE ALL

Matthew also recorded forgiveness rules.

Matt 18:32-35 Then his lord, after that he had called him, said unto him, O thou wicked servant, I forgave thee all that debt, because thou desiredst me: 33 Shouldest not thou also have had compassion on thy fellowservant, even as I had pity on thee? 34 And his lord was wroth, and delivered him to the tormentors, till he should pay all that was due unto him. 35 So likewise shall my heavenly Father do also unto you, if ye from your hearts forgive not every one his brother their trespasses. KJV

"We should take time to think about the massive job of forgiveness God has."

After giving his only Son to die for our sins that should have been enough to convince us of how important forgiveness is to God. He forgives us of all our many, many sins and failures. Perhaps then forgiving someone for not calling your name or not giving you credit or not visiting you when you were sick will come easier to your heart.

FORGIVE
~FORGIVE MEN THEIR TRESPASSES
~SEEK THE FORGIVENESS OF THY BROTHER

In your everyday experiences with men offenses are almost unavoidable. The challenge increases in areas where we have been hurt before and as a result may be very sensitive. Occasions will come when you will have to say sincerely from your heart...

"I'm sorry, it was my fault, please forgive me." Or
"I forgive you, no heart feelings."

It is at that very moment you will need to have forgiveness available to you. You may want to practice saying this statement to someone you are close to. It is more likely that you will offend someone close to you than you would offend a stranger.

It is most likely that we are more easily offended by those we love.

When you practice asking for forgiveness or forgiving someone you may discover how unfamiliar this statement is to say. A heart ready to minister is a heart that is familiar with forgiving others of trespasses and offenses.

"There are many times that unforgiveness sneaks up on us and we are unaware that we have it."

There are ways to detect unforgiveness in our hearts. If unforgiveness is not attended to it breeds and reproduces other ungodly characteristics. If you detect these attributes in your character and tendencies you may have a root of unforgiveness. Here is a list of some of the fruit from unforgiveness.

"Out of unforgiveness comes ungodly relatives: sinful cousins if you will..."

Bitterness
Hatred
Resentment
Self-pity
Low self-esteem
Prejudice
Self righteousness

Jealousy

Envy

Strife

Uncooperative spirit

Unloving spirit

Revenge

Murder

Rage, and much more!

All of these have roots or are founded upon unforgiveness. If you battle with some of these ungodly characteristics or tendencies you may need to forgive someone in your past or present and be free from the fruit of unforgiveness.

"So keep an eye out for these cousins; for at the root of this family tree you are bound to find unforgiveness."

Understand how important it is to forgive. Start with the "will" or desire to forgive. You must want to forgive and become forgiving by nature. Study the word of God about forgiving and plant a seed for forgiveness in your heart. Pray for forgiveness and a spirit to forgive. By faith in God's word, act on the power of forgiveness. Acts of kindness, gentleness, charity, love and goodness toward that person or those persons who have offended you can guard against unforgiveness reappearing once you have forgiven. But total freedom comes when you confess and repent before God. He'll give you the power to forgive!

~FORGIVE~
(For peace's sake and for heaven's sake)
Let's condition our spirits to be forgiving by practicing the Word of God.

Matt 6:14-15 For if ye forgive men their trespasses, your heavenly Father will also forgive you: 15 But if ye forgive not men their trespasses, neither will your Father forgive your trespasses. KJV

Luke 11:4 And forgive us our sins; for we also forgive every one that is indebted to us. And lead us not into temptation; but deliver us from evil. KJV

Luke 17:4 And if he trespass against thee seven times in a day, and seven times in a day turn again to thee, saying, I repent; thou shalt forgive him. KJV

Now let us explore the unpaved trail in forgiveness that will cause us to seek out our brother and cure his/her ought.

Matt 5:23-24 Therefore if thou bring thy gift to the altar, and there rememberest that thy brother hath ought against thee; 24 Leave there thy gift before the altar, and go thy way; first be reconciled to thy brother, and then come and offer thy gift. KJV

"Yes my sister and my brother, there may come a time that being clear with God will be important enough to you that you will seek out that offended one and make things right."

Then you can be right with God! So, go ahead and do the right things...FORGIVE!

THE HEART OF MINISTRY = A FORGIVING HEART

Notes:

Part II

A.

The heart that desires
to please God...

~is seeking the Lord for her/his area of ministry
~is totally surrendered to God's instructions and directions

Prov 16:7 When a man's ways please the LORD, he maketh even his enemies to be at peace with him. KJV

There are many amazing outcomes that result as we live to please God. Just as the scripture in Proverbs tells us, when we please God our enemies become at peace with us.

"This is only one of the benefits."

We will discuss more about the results as we explore the concept of pleasing God.

It is a great ambition to want to please God. It is a mandatory condition of the HEART for those who are called according to His purpose.

THE HEART READY FOR MINISTRY = POSSESS THE AMITION AND GOAL TO PLEASE GOD

Pleasing God:

To please God is to make him happy or give him pleasure. Therefore to live to please God is to live in a way that daily brings pleasure to the Father.

"So it would be pertinent to know what it is that pleases God."

Should one observe the testimonies of many of the people in the bible we can get a vivid understanding of what pleases God.

John 8:28-29 Then said Jesus unto them, When ye have lifted up the Son of man, then shall ye know that I am he, and that I do nothing of myself; but as my Father hath taught me, I speak these things. 29 And he that sent me is with me: the Father hath not left me alone; for I do always those things that please him. KJV

Jesus is our greatest example of a vessel that pleases God. He was a faithful, mission focused and obedient servant of God. He considered God in all his decisions, circumstances, commitments, and daily walk. He pleased God even to his death. He was obedient even to the cross the scriptures say. (Philippians 2:8) There were many before and after Christ who had the testimony that they pleased God. We take these examples and models to help us give God pleasure. So what should we do? We go to the word of God! What do we need to please God?

Heb 11:6 But without faith it is impossible to please him: for he that cometh to God must believe that he is, and that he is a rewarder of them that diligently seek him. KJV

"FAITH, one of the most important things we need to please God."

Faith is so essential to our walk with God that it is powerfully stated that without faith it is impossible to please God. What is faith? (See Hebrews 11:1) In fact the entire eleventh chapter of Hebrews is dedicated to those who have testimonies of faith and how they acquired that testimony.

Faith is the power to absolutely believe God will do what he promised in His word.

Faith is provided by God to every believer. It is part of the benefits package when we join the family of God.

"It is distributed by God in measures that are then expected to be increased by the individual."

The bible says we are to build up our most holy faith.

Jude 20-21 But ye, beloved, <u>building up yourselves on your most holy faith,</u> praying in the Holy Ghost, 21 Keep yourselves in the love of God, looking for the mercy of our Lord Jesus Christ unto eternal life. KJV

Rom 12:3 For I say, through the grace given unto me, to every man that is among you, not to think of himself more highly than he ought to think; but to think soberly, according as God hath dealt to every man the measure of faith. KJV

Every man has been given a measure of faith from God. This is what I would like to call "starter faith." This is the measure that God gave you to start with. It was measured out by the Lord God, thereby totally sufficient for your needs.

"Every mountain or valley that is challenging your life, can be overcome by little ol' you."

You can be assured that you are equipped to overcome, simply because God knew how much (starter) faith to measure out to you.

"Your job now is to use it and increase it."

How do you use faith? Work! (See James 2:17,20,26)

James 2:17-26 Even so faith, if it hath not works, is dead, being alone. 18 Yea, a man may say, Thou hast faith, and I have works: shew me thy faith without thy works, and I will shew thee my faith by my works. 19 Thou believest *that there is one God; thou doest well: the devils also believe, and tremble. 20 But wilt thou know, <u>O vain man, that faith without works is dead</u>? 21 Was not Abraham our father justified by works, when he had offered Isaac his son upon the altar? 22 Seest thou how faith wrought with his works, and by works was faith made perfect? 23 And the scripture was fulfilled which saith, Abraham believed God, and it was imputed unto him for righteousness: and he was called the Friend of God. 24 Ye see then how that by works a man is justified, and not by faith only. 25 Likewise also was not Rahab the harlot justified by works, when she had received the messengers, and had sent them out another way? 26 <u>For as the body without the spirit is dead, so faith without works is dead also</u>. KJV*

Faith needs to be worked. If it sits with nothing to do, it dies. Our assignment is to take what you have and work for the Lord and let him use your faith to get his plan accomplished. Display your faith through your godly works. Help the helpless, support God's causes, show kindness to a stranger, give to the poor, clothe the naked. Whatever your work is, do it as unto the glory of God. (see Colossians 3:23)

"Take a look at the news, your prayer ministry is a way to use your faith."

Pray for peace, pray for solutions, pray for justice, for your prayer of faith the bible says will save the sick.

James 5:15 And the prayer of faith shall save the sick, and the Lord shall raise him up; and if he have committed sins, they shall be forgiven him. KJV

There is no mystery to building up your most holy faith. God has made it clear and we just have to follow his instructions.

"Faith is believing that God will absolutely do what he promised he would in his word."

Therefore knowing the word is important to faith building. Romans ten provides the simple formula for increasing faith.

Rom 10:17 So then faith cometh by hearing, and hearing by the word of God. KJV

Hearing the word of God, through all of God's many means of delivering his word, increases our faith. The word of God the Holy Bible is the cultivating power for our faith. Read it, listen to it, meditate on it, or sing it in a song. Whatever way or means you choose to cultivate and grow you faith, do it by <u>hearing the word</u>. Hearing the word is not just an ear activity. It is more so a HEART activity.

THE HEART OF MINISTRY = ENGAGES THE POWER OF FAITH THROUGH THE WORD

When the heart gets involved with the Word of God, lives are changed and relationships with God become intimate and alive! Get your heart involved with God's word...INCREASE YOUR FAITH!

Now that we understand pleasing God a little clearer in our walk, let's please him in our calling. What is your area of ministry? If you are resigned in being a bench warmer you are not pleasing God.

"THERE ARE NO POSITIONS IN GOD THAT REQUIRE YOU TO SOLELY BE AN OBSERVER FROM THE CHURCH BENCH."

God is not calling us unto salvation to become members of the pews, but members of the body of Christ. This membership has only active members. If you are not an active member you should be frantically seeking god for your area of ministry. Be mindful that ministry often changes as we grow in God. So anticipate your assignment of ministry to change and evolve as you grow in the grace and knowledge of our Lord and Savior, Jesus Christ. It is of great importance that you seek to minister to the Lord, even if it is only your starting point.

"Ministry is active membership in the body of Christ."

Rather than simply occupying a position on a bench, you are occupying a position in the purpose of God's eternal plan. Then you are pleasing God.

There are many shifts and turns in a person's ministry. When I first got saved I was a devotional/praise leader. I served at my local church and as the state youth devotional team leader. Soon Sunday school teacher was added to my assignment. Then church janitor, usher, evening prayer leader was added to the list, so on and so forth. In the beginning many things were added with very few things removed. Later as I matured in God and was baptized in the Holy Ghost my area of ministry shifted and became more focused. I always remained available to work in the early ministry assignments, but a main focus of ministry rose to the top and took first place in my life. I became a missionary, a carrier of the word of God. I had received the ministry calling of evangelism and "missionary" was my starting assignment for training. I trained and practiced to fulfill that area of ministry within my calling and use my measure of faith to do a good work.

I have for quite a while seen the calling and the ministry assignment as two different stages of pleasing God. I see the calling as a specific purpose of God for my life. It's that call that Samuel heard while he was being trained under Eli. He was already active in a ministry area as a servant in the temple of God. His mother gave him to the church in gratitude to God for blessing her with a child she so desperately desired. It was assigned to him and he embraced that assignment and served in dedication and excellence. But one night he heard the call of God. He was called to be a priest and a prophet. (See 1 Samuel chapter 3) The story of Samuel's call is typical; he was found working and then was called to his specific ministry area. In my experience with those seeking their ministry area, too often individuals want to skip the servant stage of training and experience that God has as his pattern for those who surrender to their calling. The pattern is that the believer is found working in an assignment to support an existing, local work of God, at a church, mission or other environment. Then as that person develops faithful service they seem to hear the call of God that is often to be established right where they are and then spread into other areas. The HEART of ministry is to serve as God has need.

THE HEART OF MINISTRY = A SERVANT'S HEART IS OPENED TO BE USED OF GOD WHEREEVER NEEDED.

The calling is our specific assigned purpose in God's redemption plan and our ministry area is our current setting for "pleasing works" as we are working our faith to please God. As a Sunday school teacher, for example my calling would be teacher, but my area of ministry would be that local ministry and my assigned class of students.

"Callings mature, but don't often change yet they can expand and contract as God sees fit."

For example your audience may grow or the subject you teach may be more narrow or focused. There are some very powerful evangelists who once traveled the world with the message of Christ. Today you may find them centrally located within a particular subject area or function as mentors to other upcoming vessels of God. They are nonetheless evangelists, but their area of ministry has changed. Many remain evangelists and travel in more particular circles for a specific purpose. Some evangelists may find themselves as organization leaders or pastors in later seasons. The change is not lower or higher, just different according to the need or assignment of God for the season. If we reflect on Paul's ministry assignments we will see that he often spent time in a certain place specifically for the ministry to that group or location. Once his purpose was served he set someone over that church and traveled on. He remained overseer and visited and advised as needed. (See Romans 1:1-7, I Corinthians 1:1, II Corinthians 1:1, Galatians 1:1)

Waiting on your ministry does not always reflect age as much as seasons. Seasons are set times for particular things to occur. Likewise our areas of ministry shift and change as we grow and as the purpose of God requires us to reposition and serve. Those same areas of ministry and assignments will produce negative responses in our lives if we fail to grow an as required by God.

"If God is the breathe of life, then life should be in our ministry."

The most popular negative result to a stagnant, lifeless ministry is often just a lack of effectiveness. The price of a lifeless ministry is often manifested in self-righteous, harsh and abrupt behaviors that take away the glory of God from the work.

Paul began is ministry as an intern to Ananias. He quickly shifted to evangelist as he was sent by God to the gentiles.

Acts 9:15-16 But the Lord said unto him, Go thy way: for he is a chosen vessel unto me, to bear my name before the Gentiles, and kings, and the children of Israel: 16 For I will shew him how great things he must suffer for my name's sake. KJV

After Paul obeyed God in his calling as evangelist he began to establish churches in the places that received him and believers were converted unto God. He then added apostle to his assignment list, as one who establishes ministries/churches. He was no less an evangelist (his calling), but his area of ministry shifted to not only preaching the gospel to the saving of souls, but also to the establishing of churches to nurture and grow those souls won to Christ. He then had to engage in the setting up of authorities, teaching of church structure, and all other duties of an overseer of multiple churches (bishop). This mind you is the same evangelist who spent time at Ananias' house for training.

The will of God for each of us is that we work our faith in an area of ministry. If you love music, work in the area of music ministry. If you are very compassionate, work in the area of care for the sick and elderly. If you love children, work in youth ministry or be a Sunday school teacher. God's will is that you show your faith by your works. The best place to start is where there is a need, in an area of your gift. I f you are qualified or just willing to fill the gap, that's the place to begin. Remember, very few stay where they start, but starting is required. SHOW GOD YOUR FAITH!

THE HEART OF MINISTRY = A LIFE THAT DEMONSTRATES THE POWER OF FAITH IN GOD!

One tiny detail that often discourages newcomers in ministry, and that is that most need areas in churches and organizations are not very glamorous positions.

"Humble servants are not bothered, but some zealous newcomers become impatient with assignments that seem insignificant."

But there are no insignificant assignments when they support and promote the plan and purpose of God. To be honest there aren't many assignments in the body of Christ that is really considered glamorous. The glorification in ministry is revealed at heaven's judgment and not on earth. But your desire to please God overrides what seems to be an unattractive are of ministry. You are transformed into a vessel "meet for the master's use" by your desire to please your God! Surrender to your current are of ministry. If you are worried about being overlooked and not given due credit, don't worry God keeps good records of his servants and knows and sees all. Don't focus on the recognition of men and know that God pleasers do all as to the Lord.

Eph 6:6-7 Not with eyeservice, as menpleasers; but as the servants of Christ, doing the will of God from the heart;7 With good will doing service, as to the Lord, and not to men:KJV

When God was teaching me and reworking the spirit of pleasing him into my vessel I had to learn this scripture.

There have been many lessons that God had to review and renew in me that had been dulled over time. You probably can or will testify to the same. During that season God gave me a song that says, "Jesus, you've done so much for me, I'll do anything for you."

"He put it in me to sing that song to him until I really meant it."

When I occasionally waiver in my "anything" for God, I sing that song. No matter what God's instruction require or his directions cause you to encounter, surrender to the "anything for God" commitment. Then you truly are living to please God. Jesus surrendered to the "anything for God" that began at his birth and ended at the resurrection. Steven surrendered to his "anything for God" ministry at the point of being stoned to death. David surrendered to "anything for God" from a shepherd to being king over a chosen people. What will you surrender your "anything for God" to do? What will you be willing to do for God?... ANYTHING?!

Phil 1:15-21 Some indeed preach Christ even of envy and strife; and some also of good will: 16 The one preach Christ of contention, not sincerely, supposing to add affliction to my bonds: 17 But the other of love, knowing that I am set for the defense of the gospel. 18 What then? notwithstanding, every way, whether in pretence, or in truth, Christ is preached; and I therein do rejoice, yea, and will rejoice. 19 For I know that this shall turn to my salvation through your prayer, and the supply of the Spirit of Jesus Christ, 20 According to my earnest expectation and my hope, that in nothing I shall be ashamed, but that with all boldness, as always, so now also Christ shall be magnified in my body, whether it be by life, or by death. 21 For to me to live is Christ, and to die is gain. KJV

Paul put it so nicely, that he would do ANYTHING for God.

Notes:

B.

Pause for a study of "Total Surrender."

Surrendering to God is part of giving our will to God to allow him to do what he desires in our lives. The "Yes Lord" statement is also a prayer, praise, song and state of mind.

"Surrendering to the Lord is the state of mind and the heart of the believer."

In worship we often hear these words in connection to a totally surrendered vessel. Someone has chosen to give up all for the cause of God. Those two short words can transform a believer from one lowly state, to a closer place in God. If with a sincere heart a soul cries out a surrender prayer to the Lord, it positions himself/herself to be changed. Another benefit of surrender is gaining heaven. When we yield to God's will for our life, we are preparing for heaven. God loves the surrendered vessel. Let's hear a word on surrender to increase our faith.

THE HEART OF MINISTRY=GIVING UP ALL FOR THE CAUSE OF GOD

Ps 34:18 The LORD is nigh unto them that are of a broken heart; and saveth such as be of a contrite spirit. KJV

Ps 51:17 The sacrifices of God are a broken spirit: a broken and a contrite heart, O God, thou wilt not despise. KJV

Isa 57:15 For thus saith the high and lofty One that inhabiteth eternity, whose name is Holy; I dwell in the high and holy place, with him also that is of a contrite and humble spirit, to revive the spirit of the humble, and to revive the heart of the contrite ones. KJV

Isa 66:2 For all those things hath mine hand made, and those things have been, saith the LORD: but to this man will I look, even to him that is poor and of a contrite spirit, and trembleth at my word. KJV

The contrite and humble are those who have surrendered to the Almighty God. The secret that they hold is the knowledge of the power and might of the living God.

"They understand their powerlessness without him and respond likewise." Total Surrender!

In her book, <u>How to know the Will of God for Your Life</u>, Dr. Fay Ellis Butler teaches the powerful element of consecration in the life of a totally surrendered vessel. There is a need for emphasis on the sacrifice of selfish desires that are traded for actions of commitment and reliance upon God.

Consecration – To make or declare to be sacred by certain ceremonies or rites; to appropriate to sacred uses; to set apart or dedicate as holy. – To devote a sacred or high purpose; to dedicate; as, he consecrated his life to the glory of the Lord.

Dr. Butler divided areas of consecration into two parts: Personal and Entire. Personal consecration are actions taken in accordance with your will to yield to the Lord. Total Surrender!

2 Cor 8:5 And this they did, not as we hoped, but first gave their own selves to the Lord, and unto us by the will of God. KJV

Judges 5:2 Praise ye the LORD for the avenging of Israel, when the people willingly offered themselves. KJV

Once personal consecration and surrender has taken place in the will, it grows into a total surrender that Dr. Butler calls entire consecration. She gave reference to this scripture in Philippians 3.

Phil 3:7-8 But what things were gain to me, those I counted loss for Christ. 8 Yea doubtless, and I count all things but loss for the excellency of the knowledge of Christ Jesus my Lord: for whom I have suffered the loss of all things, and do count them but dung, that I may win Christ, KJV

The totally surrendered vessel has told God yes in all areas of his/her life. Is there an area in your life that you still haven't yielded to God? Many peopled overlook areas of their time, money, gifts and talents when they surrender to God.

"It is more than an emotion of sorrow, the "Yes Lord" is an ultimate surrender of our lives."

The more you say it, the more you will it. The more you will it, the more you yield it! SAY, YES TO THE LORD!

TOTAL SURRENDER! ~ YES LORD!

Surrender – 1. To yield to the power of another; to give or deliver up possession of upon compulsion of demand; as to surrender one's person to an enemy; to surrender a fort or a ship. 2. To yield, especially voluntarily, in favor of another; to resign in favor of another; to cease to claim of use; as to surrender a right or privilege; to surrender a place or an office.

Surrender – 1. To yield; to give up oneself into the power or control of another.

What are You saying when you say Yes Lord?
~Is it a word of substance or a word of tradition or habit?
Are you totally surrendered to the Lord?

~In yourself: mind, soul, body

~In your home: spouse, children, possessions

~In your job: Do you "give to caesar what is due him? How is your conduct at work?

~Before the world: Are you letting your light so shine before men?

Matthew 5:16

~In your ministry: consecration, obedience, faithfulness

THE HEART OF MINISTRY = GIVING GOD YOUR YES!

Yes to your way Lord – however you want to do things

Yes to your will Lord – whatever you want to do

I SURRENDER ALL!

Notes:

C.

The heart that is yielded and opened to God

~taking the limits off what we will/can do for God
~giving God the issues of submission
~getting the "I'll do anything for you Lord" spirit

"The weapon most useful against feelings of inadequacy and inability is acknowledging God's power."

What God does in us and through us makes us effective instruments for his purpose. Taking the limits off of what we will or can do for God comes easiest to those who realize that "Power belongeth to God!"

Ps 62:11 God hath spoken once; twice have I heard this; that power belongeth unto God. KJV

Phil 4:13 I can do all things through Christ which strengtheneth me. KJV

Gal 2:20 I am crucified with Christ: nevertheless I live; yet not I, but Christ liveth in me: and the life which I now live in the flesh I live by the faith of the Son of God, who loved me, and gave himself for me. KJV

2 Cor 3:5-6 Not that we are sufficient of ourselves to think any thing as of ourselves; but our sufficiency is of God;6 Who also hath made us able ministers of the new testament; not of the letter, but of the spirit: for the letter killeth, but the spirit giveth life. KJV

There is a treasure in the word of God that transfers self-focused behavior to God-focused behavior. Not the "I" but the focus is the Christ in the works done. To God be the glory!

THE HEART OF MINISTRY = GOD FOCUSED BEHAVIOR AND WORKS

A short look at giving God the issues of submission
~make submission to God your guide

If the scripture is true, then let the word speak.

"It is better to obey God than men."

(See Acts 5:29) If the requirement is to submit, check if it aligns with the word of God. Struggles subside when we realize that obeying God will determine our position. If we are pleasing vessels of the most high God there is no long lasting concern over the issue of submission. When we master surrender, submission comes easy.

THE HEART OF MINISTRY = A SERVANT'S SPIRIT

Often some would be fearful of surrender or submission because of previous abuses or misuses of their trust. But we should never be concerned that God would abuse or misuse us. He will never put us in the place where we are doormats or slaves. His word lets us know that we are no longer slaves but friends and sons by adoption into the powerful family of God. Some places of growth and life lessons look like places of limitations, but be assured the Lord has good in mind for you.

Jer 29:11-12 For I know the thoughts that I think toward you, saith the LORD, thoughts of peace, and not of evil, to give you an expected end. 12 Then shall ye call upon me, and ye shall go and pray unto me, and I will hearken unto you. KJV

"Submission is not a punishment."

Check the word of God, he means only what is best for you. Find out what God wants you to do and follow his guidelines in obedience. What is God requiring of you in areas of ministry and sacrifice? God has specific plans for your life and your HEARTS POSITION IN MINISTRY will dictate your pathway. Say yes to the will of God and watch him create in you a HEART of powerful ministry. Discover your current area of ministry and work your faith right there!

There was a time in my life when I grew tired of proving myself to be who God says I am. The beginning of the end of that battle for me came when God instructed me to "take my place in ministry, but never fight for my space." His word still rings in my ears and heart so clear... "Your gift will make room for you."

Prov 18:16 A man's gift maketh room for him, and bringeth him before great men. KJV

To take my place in ministry I had to be assured of my calling. It is important that there is assurance in my heart that I am saved and that I am seeking to please God in my life. When selfish desires and ambitions are erased then true ministry begins in our vessels. I have to guard my anointing with discernment of distractions that may come my way. I must focus my life on God's purpose in me and not be drawn away by men's voices of praise and approval.

"This does not mean that I won't make mistakes, but I will be conscious of the choices that I make that may impact or change my ministry availability."

So take your place, but don't fight for your space in ministry.

"Your gift will make room for you."

Then allow God to use you in your current assignment as he prepares you for future ministry. The fight for your space is when you are always seeking to prove to others that you belong where you are, or that you are qualified for the position you hold. When you aren't constantly maneuvering for the spotlight or the position of high recognition, then you are no longer fighting for your space. But be careful, this fight is never over. Keep your guards up against selfish ambitions and strive to please God.

Give God all your issues of submission.

Whether the fight is located in your home, on your job, in the line at the store, on in the church, it's still priority that we always please God."

As long as we are fighting for our space, we will not possess our rightful place. Submit yourself totally to the Lord and all the other issues will be handled for you. Don't give the enemy a weapon to use against you. Selfish ambitions, seeking acknowledgment from man, low self –esteem, and rejection can become powerful weapons against us. Depend on the power of God to set your agenda. The Holy Ghost can handle it with power!...you can't win without God.

James 4:7-10 Submit yourselves therefore to God. Resist the devil, and he will flee from you. 8 Draw nigh to God, and he will draw nigh to you. Cleanse your hands, ye sinners; and purify your hearts, ye double minded. 9 Be afflicted, and mourn, and weep: let your laughter be turned to mourning, and your joy to heaviness. 10 Humble yourselves in the sight of the Lord, and he shall lift you up. KJV

Gal 6:9 And let us not be weary in well doing: for in due season we shall reap, if we faint not. KJV

"Lord in all that we desire in this lie, we desire most to please you. Prepare our hearts to be vessels of your divine purpose. We face the truth of our past. There are times we have failed, and there are times we were not in control of things that happened to us. No matter the case, we confess our sins before you and ask for your blood to wash us. Separate us from the sin and the residue of sin that chains us to our past. We forgive those who have offended us and the offense. Therefore we seek to be free from the person and the event that has enslaved our wills. Free us by your power and deliver us quickly and totally. Our HEARTS desire is to please you. We want to give you pleasure! We are no longer ruled by past experiences and unforgiveness. We choose to have a HEART of forgiveness. We choose to forgive both the offender and the offense. Freedom replaces the bondage, peace replaces the struggle and fear, min-

istry replaces slothfulness and unconcern. Glory replaces shame. Give me a clean heart, Oh god, and renew a right spirit within me. I submit to you. I surrender all to thee. I trust you with my Heart! I freely surrender my Heart to your plan and purpose. I trust you with my future! I trust you with my life! Use me. Anoint me. Use me! Anoint me Lord! Empower me to be your servant in ministry. In Jesus' all powerful name I pray and receive today! AMEN

THE HEART OF MINISTRY IS PREPARED WHEN AREAS HAVE BEEN EXAMINED AND FOUND WITHOUT SIN AND READY TO BE USED. REMEMBER...

YOU WILL KNOW YOU HAVE THE HEART OF MINISTRY!

THE HEART = YOUR WILL

THE HEART OF MINISTRY ...
=THE CONDITION WHERE GOD CAUSES
CHANGE SO WE CAN BE USED
= THE PLACE OF TRUSTING GOD
=THE POWER OF FREEDOM THROUGH
FORGIVENESS
= EMPOWERED TO FIRGIVE ALL
=A FORGIVING HEART
= POSSESSING THE AMBITION AND GOAL TO
PLEASE GOD IN EVERYTHING
=ENGAGING THE POWER OF FAITH THROUGH
THE WORD OF GOD
=A SERVANT'S HEART THAT IS OPENED TO BE
USED OF GOD WHEREEVER NEEDED
=A LIFE THAT DEMONSTRATES THE POWER
OF FAITH IN GOD

=GIVING UP ALL FOR THE CAUSE OF GOD

= GIVING GOD YOUR YES!

=HAVING GOD FOCUSED BEHAVIOR
AND WORKS

=A SERVANT'S SPIRIT

THE HEART OF MINISTRY IS PREPARED WHEN WE HAVE BEEN EXAMINED BY GOD AND FOUND WITHOUT SIN AND READY TO BE USED FOR A HEAVENLY PURPOSE!

BIBLIOGRAPHY

All scripture references were from the King James Bible.

The Holy Bible, KJV

Called to be Saints, Butler, Fay Ellis

How to Know the Will of God for Your Life, Butler, Fay
    Ellis

Webster new Universal Unabridged Dictionary, 1972

ABOUT THE AUTHOR
Evangelist/Co-Pastor Cynthia Lynette Butler

Evangelist Cynthia Butler is CoPastor and Vice President of Joy of Life Ministries, Inc. She is the wife of Pastor Eric Butler for over 24 years and fervently supports the vision of her husband. They have been blessed with three amazing children. Sister Butler gave her life to Christ at a young age and has been serving in ministry for over thirty-five years. She has been given many opportunities to grow in ministry through the leadership of powerful men and women of God who have unselfishly mentored her. She will always be grateful. She is a sought after speaker and workshop facilitator.

Professionally, Cynthia Butler is an educator. She continues her mission as CEO and Director of the Purpose Driven Advocacy Center, Inc. which provides education and life advancing advocacy services to youth, adults and families. The Purpose Driven Advocacy Center, Inc. is a community service agency.

CoPastor Cynthia's ministry theme is "Serving God by Serving His People."

Other books by the author: "ARREST ~A formula for Deliverance"
Also ask about the 'Triple CD' set of CoPastor Cynthia teaching the ARREST revelation to the Joy of Life Bible Study.
"Preparing the HEART for Ministry" and "ARREST~A Formula for Deliverance" were taught and written to increase faith in the promises of God and faith in the power of God. Other works are in progress.

Contact Information:

CoPastor Cynthia Butler, M.S. Edu. Admin.

c/o Joy of Life Ministries, Inc.

6401 N. 56th Street, Omaha, NE 68104,

402-399-9628 or email at Evangclb@aol.com

LaVergne, TN USA
06 September 2010

195980LV00004B/3/P

Pastor Paisley
Psm 27:4

"Dwell"

We live in "Dwell".
Attitude of expectancy.
Believe without doubt.
My children live in "Dwell"

Every anointed prophetic word spoken over
me & my family, my husband, my children my seed
will multiply great fruit & set free
Tiffany – is healed & healthy delivered healing
Arthur – is healed and set free
Curl – is delivered and well established
the word of God
their walks in the children are children of light
" My children and their children are mighty men & women
of God! They are covered under the blood of Jesus they are sent
the are Kingdom builders, they all overcomers
they walk in health, wealth & prosperity
winners !!